The Any Game Cookbook

The Any Game Cookbook

Recipes for Spiritual Gaming

Claude Needham Ph.D.

Gateways Books and Tapes, Nevada City, California

ISBN-13: 978-0-89556-189-3
ISBN-10: 0-89556-189-1

Cover design by the author

Published by GATEWAYS / IDHHB, INC.
P.O. Box 370, Nevada City, CA 95959
(800) 869-0658; (530) 477-8101
http://www.gatewaysbooksandtapes.com

Library of Congress Cataloging-in-Publication Data

Needham, Claude, 1951-
The any game cookbook : recipes for spiritual gaming /
Claude W.
Needham.
p. cm.
Includes bibliographical references.
ISBN-13: 978-0-89556-189-3
ISBN-10: 0-89556-189-1
1. Spiritual life. 2. Games--Religious aspects. I. Title.
BL624.N44 2006
793--dc22
2006023774

Table of Contents

Introduction....1
What Is Any Game?....3
A Dedication....5
Recipes....7
A Note About Sequence....9
I Wish....11
Significance....13
Beads On A String....15
Goals and Aims....19
Hanging Down....23
Not So Sure....25
Getting Into A Game....27
Stage Presence....29
I Saw That....31
Making Space....33
Play With Feeling....35
Body Parts....37
In the Mirror....39
On Your Own Center....41
I Am Playing A Game....43
Effecting Others....45
I Am Here....47
World Game....49
Going A Little Macro....51
Get A Question Answered....53
Will To Play....55
Doorways....57
Left Hand, Right Hand....59
Use Alternate Hand....61
Sitting Like A Stone....63

I'm A Toy....65
Keep the Rhythm....67
Moment of Freedom....69
Be A Robot....71
Waldo....73
On Stage....75
Performance Art....77
Marionette....79
Subliminal Scenes....81
Meeting of Minds....83
By Any Other Name....85
Aura....87
Plasma Ring....89
Super Glue....91
Giants....93
Last Move....95
Friendly Strangers....97
On the Lookout....99
Post-Hypnotic Suggestion....101
Tea Party....103
Copy & Paste....105
Be Here New....107
Counting Primes....109
Tap, Tap, Tap....111
Clown Face....113
Molasses Atmosphere....115
Cloning Around....117
Reincarnation Of You....119
Negative Space....121
Take Your Turn....123
Reactions....125
Gratitude....127

Powwow....129
Don't Touch Anything....131
Feet On the Floor....133
Peek-A-Boo....135
Sit in a Box....137
Chopsticks and Socks....139
At My Back....141
Look and Listen....143
Talk To The Hand....145
Play In The Bathtub....147
Playing Elsewhere....149
Backwards....151
Relax Facial Mask....153
Deaf, Dumb, or Blind....155
Snap Shots....157
At the Adults' Table....159
Afterword....161
Notes on Sub-Vocalization....163
X-Factors....165
Homage....171
About the Author....173

Introduction

In *The Any Game Cookbook* you'll find a bountiful buffet of spiritual exercises; a veritable smörgåsbord of gaming recipes. Each recipe is designed to transform the playing of *any game* into a spiritual gaming experience.

Ordinarily playing a game is... well... um, ordinary. However, with the application of a recipe from this book, you can transform playing any of those aging games gathering dust in the hall closet into a new gaming experience—a spiritual gaming adventure.

Under normal circumstances this would be an ideal time to define what is meant by spiritual and spiritual gaming. I agree, under normal circumstances that would make perfect sense, but, alas, this is not one of those normal circumstances.

This book is intended as a door opener, an invitation for *you* to explore *your* experience, an invitation for you to take a guided tour of your spiritual nature. I have no intention of limiting your potential horizons by definitions and head-brain explanations.

If you want to compare notes after you've made a few journeys of your own, let's talk.

What Is *Any Game*?

While working on the book *Spiritual Gaming with the Classics,* it became evident that many of the suggested rule modifications would work equally well on most any game. For example, the rules designed to turn Parcheesi into a spiritual game were found to work equally well on any game played with dice and markers. This became the inspiration for *The Any Game Cookbook*—a collection of rule modifications, exercises, mentations, and assorted activities designed to turn *any game* into a spiritual adventure.

But wait, before you head off to the toy store searching the aisles for a game called "any game", let me share a bit of news: *Any Game*(tm) is in production and available for purchase. However, the game is only sold directly from the manufacturer. If you are interested in a copy of the game, contact Gateways Books and Tapes requesting a price list. I'm sure they will be happy to hook you up.

However, least you think it necessary to purchase a special game for use with this book, let me assure you that "any game" can mean literally any game–Monopoly, Canasta, Pinochle, Chess, Cribbage, Parcheesi, Domino, Ping Pong, etcetera, so forth, and so on.

A Dedication

Imagine the world of a bug living its life between two sheets of plywood. This imaginary creature would be trapped in a world of forward, backward, left, and right. That's it, just two dimensions of travel. Between sheets of plywood there would be no up or down—just left, right, forward, and backward.

Imagine that wonderful moment when our little bug friend makes its way to the edge of the plywood to emerge into a world with the new dimension of up-down. Back in the world of flat between the plywood up-down was only a myth. Up-down was something that philosophers may have guessed at. Now, much to our buggy friend's surprise, it is smack dab face-to-face with this new dimension.

How our bug reacts to this newfound freedom of up and down will depend a great deal on its ability to move within this new dimension. If the bug has wings and can fly, life will be good as it flies for the first time free with sky above and ground below. If, on the other hand, the bug has no means of flight, then the sequence of events might be something like: emerge into a new dimension, experience a new-found freedom of movement, puzzle at the strange rushing sounds of wind whipping past one's buggy ears, followed by a resounding splat on the ground below.

Most likely, our little friend would have appreciated this new-found freedom if it had some prior preparation—

suddenly going splat is not the best introduction to a new dimension.

It is to this bug that I dedicate *The Any Game Cookbook*. These recipes for transforming otherwise ordinary games into spiritual adventures are designed to exercise extradimensional muscles of movement.

Recipes

(What are they?)

Have you ever eaten a croissant or a butter cookie?

How can a little flour, sugar, a bit of butter, leavening, and a dash of salt be so yummy? I've tasted the ingredients: flour is gritty, salt a bit sandy, butter is just greasy on the tongue, and yeast is plain yucky eaten from the package. No way could one predict that these ingredients, properly combined and baked, would be so tasty.

Do yourself a favor and don't judge the spiritual gaming recipes in this book based on a simple reading of the instructions. That would be like judging a cake from reading its list of ingredients.

Cook up the recipe, and actually give it a try before you dismiss it as "not to your taste."

Bon appetite.

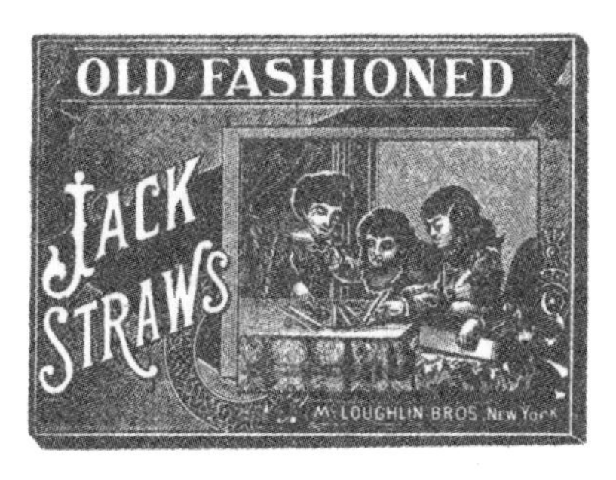

A Note About Sequence

The recipes within this book are presented in a sequence. Let's face it, this is a book. A book is a linear collection of pages bound one after the other. Just as there must be a first page and a last page, so must there also be a first recipe and a last recipe. And so we have a sequence.

However, keep in mind the sequence of recipes in this book is just *a* sequence–not *the* sequence. If you feel drawn to experiment with these recipes in a different order, please feel free–you have my permission.

It is not expected, nor required, that everyone follow the sequence of recipes as laid out in this book. Books are linear, spiritual development is not.

Try
THIS

I Wish...

Recipe) Before playing *any game*, vocalize (or sub-vocalize) the following wish: "I wish this to be used for the benefit of all beings everywhere."

In the appendices of this book you'll find a few notes on the subject of sub-vocalizations. Let me just summarize here: Don't just think the words, use your voice. It doesn't matter how loud or how soft. Just make sure you are using your voice.

When you use your voice, you will bring the wish from the domain of idle thought into the realm of active intention.

Significance

Either everything is totally significant or nothing is significant at all. Either the events of the game are ripe with meaning or they are just random blips in a cosmic Geiger counter.

Recipe 1) When playing *any game*, accept, assume, presume, assess, or just plain insist that every aspect of the game is highly significant. A die roll of two followed by a die roll five is obviously full of intense significance and ripe with meaning.

Throughout the game, be ever vigilant for the cosmic inner significance of each and every nuance of the game play.

Recipe 2) While playing *any game*, each turn remind yourself that the game is governed by random chance. The juxtaposition of events has no inner meaning other than the natural is-ness of the moment.

Even if you should roll the dice and it happens to spell out a long lost friend's phone number, this means nothing. It is pure chance and the stuff of coincidence.

Recipe 3) As you play *any game*, continue an internal dialog between you, yourself, and you on the question: "Are complete significance and total coincidence the only two options?"

Beads On A String

Consider the image of life as a single thread of experience, one end defined by the birth of this body and the other end by its inevitable death. An interesting notion, but life is really a bit lumpier than that. A common day might be composed of lumps such as: waking, morning ablutions, breakfast, driving to work, morning meeting, working at the desk, lunch, afternoon, driving home, dinner preparations, eating dinner, evening, going to bed. These are rather large lumps which could easily be broken into much smaller pieces. However, these example lumps should suffice to convey the notion that our day, and life, is composed of many, many little lumps, each having its own beginning and end.

One could picture this sequence of lumps as beads on a string, each bead representing a self-relating event with a natural beginning and natural end. In between each bead is a small transition represented by the connecting string.

It may be no surprise that *any game* can also be represented as beads on a string—each player's turn adding yet another bead to the growing strand representing the play of that game.

Recipe 1) While playing *any game*, each time your turn comes around, mark that as the beginning moment of a new bead. Then, as you finish your turn, mark that as the ending moment of the new bead. Each turn from start to finish forms a new bead—each bead independent and unique.

Recipe 2) Once again, while playing *any game*, form each turn into a separate bead by intentionally marking the beginning and end of that segment of experience. The difference in this recipe is to add the ingredient of perspective. To add perspective, visualize the complete string of beads making up the game as already finished. As you work the bead of the moment, visualize the bead of your past turn on one side and the bead of your future turn on the other side with the current bead sandwiched between beads in a complete necklace. Don't let the apparent fact that you have not as yet lived the future beads of the game cause you to visualize them with any less substance. Grant future beads and past beads equal substance.

NOTE: A necklace made from a random array of miscellaneous beads of mixed colors, size, and shape may have a certain appeal. However, a truly gorgeous necklace is composed as a symphony of coherent patterns. Small, small, large, small, small, large, blue, small, blue, tube, tube, blue, small, blue, small—each pattern gives rise to an ebb and flow of design. These necklaces can reach toward the heights of refined aesthetic or plummet to the depths of dreck. It's all in the pattern and its execution.

Recipe 3) While playing *any game,* form each of your turns into a bead. To this, add the following ingredient: View the turns of your fellow players along with your turn as beads on the necklace making up the whole of the game.

Appreciate the pattern of beads created by the round of turns. Appreciate the contribution of each player's turn and the bead it adds to the pattern of the necklace.

Recipe 4) As you play *any game,* look at each of your turns as a visitation to the same bead. Even though each turn may look different, ignore this apparent diversity. Whether it looks like it or not, for the duration of this game, each turn is the same turn. As you play, you are passing back through the same bead. As you revisit the same bead turn after turn, work it, polish it, refine it as you would a stone buffed to a fine polish, using your attention and presence.

NOTE: this recipe is best applied to a game with repetitive actions. For example, when playing Crazy Eights, each turn is more or less the same: draw a card, organize your hand, discard a card.

Goals and Aims

Each game has its own explicit goal—such as capturing your opponent's king (as in Chess), or just keeping a small white ball in movement (as in a practice rally of Ping Pong), or following the movements of a friend (as in Follow The Leader.)

Whatever the game, there will be at least one explicit, easy to understand goal. That's one of the wonderful things about games.

While playing a game, a player may take upon himself or herself any number of different internalized goals. These goals may be individual or group, altruistic or selfish. These extra goals may be short-lived or long-term. Whatever they are, there they are.

Each of us, whether we acknowledge it or not, has any number of concurrent goals running while we play.

The recipes in this section are intended to focus a spotlight on the undercurrent of goals that come and go just under the surface.

Hopefully these recipes will aid us in learning to tell ourselves the truth about our own goals and aims. In addition, it couldn't hurt to develop a capacity to voluntarize goals–take them off and put them on as we would a theater mask.

Recipe 1) During *any game,* as you finish your turn, ask the question: "What did I hope to accomplish with that?"

You are not being graded on this recipe. That means you don't need to look for the best, most correct, or accepted answer. Acknowledge whatever bubbles-up in response to the question, then move along.

Recipe 2) During *any game,* as you finish your turn, ask the question: "I wonder what I meant by that?"

Recipe 3) During *any game,* as you finish your turn, ask the question: "What was the problem for which that was a solution?"

Each of the above questions throws a slightly different light on the same basic inquiry. Try each formulation on for size.

Keep in mind that we are not necessarily looking for deep or cunning goals. Preventing my opponent's queen from capturing my bishop may be a perfectly valid answer. Or, perhaps the answer will be something more psychological like a desire to demonstrate one's cleverness. Spiritual, whimsical, rude, lewd, or just plain "biding my time until I figure out how to play this darn game". Whatever the goal, just take note and move along. This is a fact-finding mission, not yet another exercise in fault-finding or feeling guilty.

Acknowledge the answers that come up within your mental chatter–then move along. No analysis here. Just simple acknowledgment. You can't afford to get lost in analysis. After all, there is another turn coming up in just a moment or two.

Recipe 4) While playing *any game*, each turn try on a goal in addition to whatever goals the game dictates. Then, during that given turn, do your best to have that turn serve the selected goal.

Maybe the selected goal is "annoy my opponent," "make my opponent feel well-disposed toward me," or "bring a little chaos into the game." Whatever the selected goal, put it "on". To the best of your ability, have the current turn serve that goal.

If you happen to have a set of *Spiritual Gaming Goal Cards*, draw one from the deck before each turn.

Recipe 5) During *any game*, as your opponent plays out his or her turn, ask the question: "What do they hope to accomplish with this move?"

Recipe 6) During *any game*, as your opponent plays out his or her turn, ask the question: "I wonder what they mean by that?"

Recipe 7) During *any game*, as your opponent plays out his or her turn, ask the question: "What is the problem for which this is a solution?"

Hanging Down

Recipe) While playing *any game,* take on, nurture, and hold the notion that you are hanging upside down from the floor, with your head dangling down toward the ceiling.

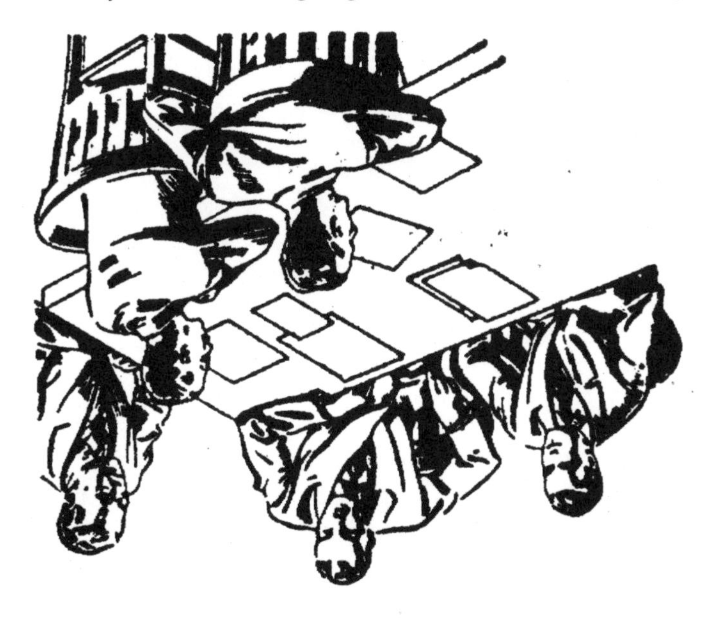

Perhaps you've heard the expression "just hanging out." Well, in this recipe we are "just hanging down."

Hint: To help remember, it might help to create a reminding factor. You can do this by linking your wish to keep this intention to a repetitive action in the game.

For example, each time you roll the dice, you could remind yourself that you are hanging upside down from the floor with your head dangling down toward the ceiling. Select something and use that as an occasion to remind yourself that no matter what it looks like, "in truth, you are hanging upside down."

Not So Sure

Recipe 1) As you play *any game,* don't be so sure about who you are. Open the doorway to the possibility that you may not be who you think you are. Just don't be so damn sure about the certainty of it all.

Recipe 2) As you play *any game,* don't be so sure about where you are. Entertain a breath of suspicion that you might not be where you think you are.

Recipe 3) As you play *any game,* don't be so sure about who you are with. Don't get all straight-jacket paranoid on everyone. Just consider it as a possibility that your fellow game players may not be who you think they are.

There are plenty of science fiction movies, both good and bad, that have explored these themes. Some of my favorites are the old black and white episodes of Twilight Zone. There is one I recall in which the protagonist (our hero) wakes in bed with his wife. Trouble is, he doesn't recall being married, he doesn't *feel* married, and the bedroom does not feel like his bedroom. In the story, it turns out he was indeed "not from around here."

In these recipes, allow yourself to entertain the inner notion that you may be awakening, partially, from a hypnotic dream–and that you are, in fact, not really who you have been induced into thinking you are.

Since you have no idea how long you have been under this

hypnotic suggestion, and you have no idea what is really going on, it might be a good idea to stay awake and pay attention. Gather a little evidence about this odd circumstance you find yourself in—see if you can pick up a clue or two about what is going on.

Getting Into A Game

There is a simple ploy I've found useful as a door opener into alternate perspectives—treat a common expression as if literal. For example, the expression "get into it"—typically meaning to become deeply involved—when taken literally, becomes a prescription to climb into a game like a test pilot climbing into an airplane cockpit.

Recipe) As you play *any game,* take on, nurture, and hold the notion that somehow you are a participant in an eternal game without beginning and without end.

Normally when sitting down to play a game, we have the perspective that we are the same (constant) individual and that we are changing our activity. For this recipe, we use the perspective that the game is constant and it is us that changes to slip into the pre-existing game.

One perspective: We are always the same—yesterday, today, and tomorrow—and it is the activities we do that changes. Another perspective: The game is always the same—eternal unchanging, persistent—and it is the participants that change.

This means that rather than starting a new game at the beginning of this evening's game, you are "getting into" a pre-existing game that was already in progress. And, when the game ends, you are simply stepping out of the game which continues creating a vacancy to be filled by another.

Your task is to play well while it is your time, and to step out with elegance when your time is up. Make it your job, as a participant in this eternal game, to play your part well while it is your time.

There are two ways to approach this game session:

Method 1) During a gaming session, use the perspective that you are a temporary visitor in a game that has been ongoing since the beginning of time and that your fellow players are, in reality, complete strangers. You only seem to know these people because the game tells you that you know these people. It is only a by-product of being within the game that seduces you into the false belief that you know the others involved. This self-induced hallucination is complete with invented histories and implanted memories of shared experiences.

Method 2) During a gaming session, use the perspective that you and your friends have known each other since the beginning of time and have just now slipped into the game session as a group. Previously, each of you were somewhere else doing something else. Now you are all inhabiting various forms within this continuing game.

Both of these methods are productive in different ways.

Stage Presence

Stage presence is something best observed by its sudden absence. I've had occasion to notice this while watching a performance from the wings of the stage. A performer will exit the stage, then, after leaving the view of the audience, they will drop their stage presence. Something will slip from their countenance, and suddenly, the actor will be his or her "street-self."

While holding a stage presence, a performer's carriage, posture, tone, attitude, and way of being is *on*. One can sense that they know they are being watched, and that it matters what they do, and how they do it.

A fun exercise that some actors engage in is to move props about the stage with and without stage presence. The results of this are visible and feelable.

If you have any question about the nature of stage presence, ask around at your local play troop, theatrical department, or pay attention next time you see a performance.

Recipe) While playing *any game*, maintain your stage presence.

I Saw That

Many of the recipes in this book can be used invisibly. No one but you needs know you are doing anything other than playing a game. On the other hand, some of the recipes require that you either have a very tolerant group of friends, or that they are participating in the recipe. This is one of those type recipes.

Recipe) While playing *any game,* after your opponent (co-player) makes her game move, inform her of what she did during her turn. After your summary, your co-player would acknowledge your observation.

Consider the following sample from an imaginary game:

Co-player: Rolls dice and moves her piece six squares.

You: "You just moved six squares."

Co-player: "Yes, that is what I did."

You: Roll dice and move your piece three squares.

Co-player: "You just moved your piece three squares."

You: "Yes, I did."

Proceed thus throughout the game. When playing with more than two, have the player whose turn is coming next comment upon the move of the preceding player.

Don't let the odd nature of this recipe deter you from giving it a try. Given an attitude and proper introduction, this recipe could be fun with the kids, or most anyone with a vestigial sense of fun. There was nothing said about making your observations with the conversational tone of a robot. When playing with kids, you could use an excited, appreciative, or complimentary voice.

Making Space

Recipe) When playing *any game*, make space for your move before making it. That move may be rolling the dice, spinning a spinner, drawing a card, moving your piece, or arranging tiles. Whatever action the game requires, just before making your move, clear the space of hurry and the need to be elsewhere. Make it very much okay that making your move in this game is exactly what you should be doing at this moment. There is nowhere else you should be and there is nothing else you should be doing. Expand that moment, allow it to permeate the space like the scent of a perfume filling a room. This *is* what you should be doing at this moment. Now, make your move.

"This is where I am..."

"This is what I am doing..."

"I am here doing it..."

"Here goes..."

Then make the leap into now and do your move.

If during the process of trying to make space for your move you discover that you really can't give yourself permission to not be somewhere else, then stop playing the game and go do whatever else is so darn important. It might be very true that there is something else you should be doing. Tell yourself the truth and just go do it.

However, if you can't be somewhere else doing whatever was so important, and you are stuck playing the game, stop fighting it and play the game. Make space to play the game. By your own admission, you are stuck. There might be somewhere else that you should be, but you can't be there, so make the space to be where you are.

In the words of local vernacular: "Either perform your biologically-dictated elimination functions, or get off the culturally-accepted ceramic receptacle for bodily waste."

Play With Feeling

Recipe) When playing *any game*, before each turn, draw a "feeling" card from your *Spiritual Gaming Mood Deck*. Then, make your game move while expressing the mood/feeling indicated by the card.

NOTE: If you do not have a *Spiritual Gaming Mood Deck*, you can approximate such a deck by writing various feelings and moods on blank business cards. If you want an official Mood Deck, contact the publisher.

Body Parts

Recipe) When playing *any game*, draw a card from your Spiritual Gaming Body Parts Deck before each turn. Then, during your normal game move, split attention between awareness of the indicated body part and making the game move. Just play the game as normal while maintaining a portion of your attention on the indicated body part.

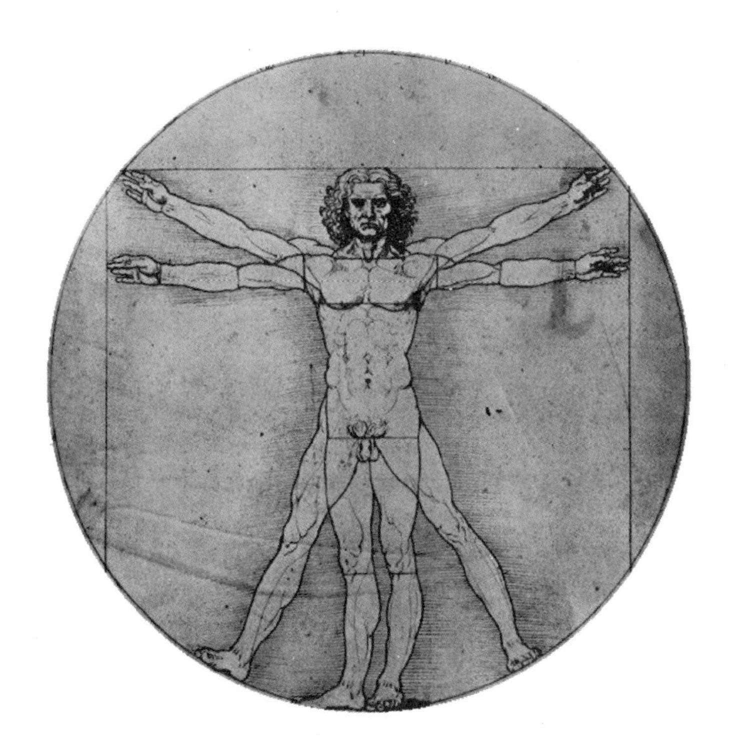

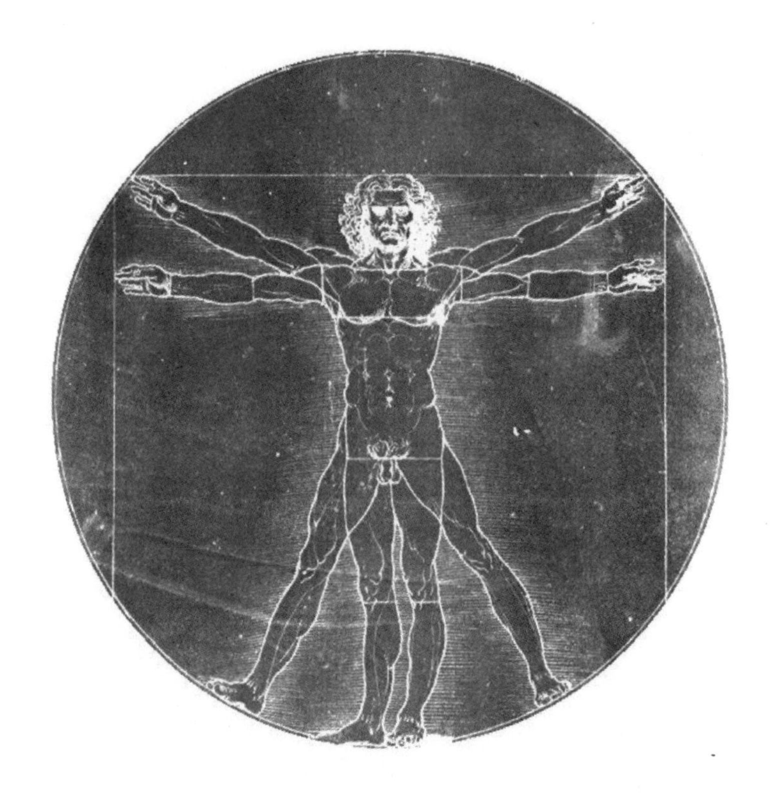

NOTE: If you do not have a *Spiritual Gaming Body Parts Deck*, you can approximate such a deck by writing various body parts on blank business cards. "Foot, leg, hand, back, head, etc."

In the Mirror

You may have encountered in literature or movies the notion that there is a whole world within a mirror—a whole world on the other side of the glass. The idea being that if only there were some way to cross the threshold of the mirror's glass, we could enter a whole world—a mirror world of this one.

We tend to think of the world on the other side of the mirror as the duplicate world or the counterfeit world. We think of it as the shadow of this world. But what if that is not the whole of the story.

What if we are that world? What if we are the ones on the other side of the mirror? What if we are the reflected ones?

Recipe) While playing *any game,* remind yourself periodically that you and the game you are participating in, are the reflections of another you playing the actual game.

On Your Own Center

Recipe) Get a sense of being where you are. By this I mean, if you are sitting on a chair at the game table, feel the chair beneath you. Get a total sense of sitting on that chair, on that two feet by two feet parcel of earth. Feel the ground and chair below you supporting you totally. Feel the earth pushing back as you push down. Sit (or stand) your ground. That is your piece of real estate.

For me, it helps to feel the connecting interface between me and where I am. I start by feeling my bottom-side pressed into the cushion of the chair. I notice the cushion pushing back, feel the solid support. Then I feel my feet touching the floor and the floor touching my feet.

After establishing contact with the ground below, I get a sense of the surrounding air pressed up against my skin as the skin presses back.

To round out the recipe, add a dash of "visualizing where my current piece of real estate is." See the chair at the table, see the table in the living room, see the living room in the apartment, on the floor, in the building, on the block, in the city, on the planet. Do all of this quickly.

Leave a small portion of your attention on this process then shift the major portion to concentrate fully on being in the spot where you are.

After all of this is running, make your game move.

I Am Playing A Game

Recipe) Each turn of the game, remind yourself: "I am playing a game."

Sub-vocalize the phrase each turn. That means don't just think the words, use your voice. It doesn't matter how loud or how soft. Just make sure you are using your voice.

As you say, "I am playing a game", you may or may not have thoughts, feelings, or what-have-you ripple about in response to the sub-vocalization. Don't be attracted nor repelled by these random bits.

This is not philosophy. You don't win a prize for the quantity, or even the quality, of ideas stimulated by this mentation. At the same time, you need not be fearsome of ideas. There is no prize and there is no penalty.

This is not psychology. You don't win a prize for the degree of spin or depth of tweak brought about by this sub-vocalization. At the same time, you need not dread the prospect that some things may come up in response to the sub-vocalization. There is no prize and there is no penalty.

This is not a soap opera. You don't need to look for or run away from melodrama. It is neither wanted nor rejected.

During the game, as your turn comes around, simply state: "I am playing a game." Don't just repeat the phrase like a somnambulistic robot. Put some energy into it.

Like dropping a pebble into a pond, each repetition of the phrase will bring ripples. That is the nature of things. These ripples are neither good nor bad. They just are.

Affecting Others

Recipe 1) While playing *any game*, during your turn, take a moment to reflect on the affect your move has on the other players in the game. As you make your move, sense the affect it has on others.

None of us live in a vacuum. This is especially true in a game where each turn our moves change the playing field of the game. Each turn, when your fellow players make their moves, the game is different for them because of what you have done during your turn.

When you add a hotel to Boardwalk, suddenly your fellow players are moving on a different landscape. If you move your bishop on the chess board, then your opponent is looking at a new situation with shifted lines of power and development. Each turn you take, each move you make affects all of those in the game.

Be aware as you make your move, that the move you make is having an affect upon others.

Another, perhaps preparatory version of this recipe, could be used to lay the foundation for the above recipe.

Recipe 2) When playing *any game,* repeat something like the following at the beginning of each turn.

"I am not in this by myself. There are others here. I am here with Sally, Frank, George, and John. We are all playing this game together."

You will, of course, need to replace the sample names with those of whomever is playing with you.

I Am Here

Recipe) Each turn of the game remind yourself: "I am here."

As you resonate "I", follow the arrow back to the who-ness of you. As you resonate "am", take note of your intention to be. As you resonate "here", sense where you are.

If this recipe makes no sense, not to worry. Come back to it from time to time and test it out. After working on many of the other recipes in this book, a day will come when suddenly this recipe will not only make sense, you may have the equipment necessary to actually do the recipe.

EXTRA!

World Game

Recipe) While playing *any game*, before making your game move, take a moment to see yourself at the table.

Step back one click and see yourself, your fellow players, and the table in the room.

Step back one click and see the room in a building.

Step back one click to see that building on a block.

Step back one click to see that block in a city.

Step back one click to see that city in a county.

Step back one click to see that county in a state.

Step back one click to see that state in a country.

Step back one click to see that country on a continent.

Step back one click to see that continent in the world.

Step back one click to see the planet as part of the solar system.

Step back one click to see the solar system as part of a galaxy.

Step back one click to see that galaxy as part of a super galaxy.

Step back one click to see that super galaxy as part of a cosmos.

Come back into the game space sitting at the table about to make your move—then make your move.

Going A Little Macro

Geography is not the only measure of position. We live in more than a three-dimensional world. Height, width, and depth are not the only dimensions in which we find ourselves. Ambiance is another dimension through which we can move.

Recipe) Before making your game move, take careful note of the ambiance of the space you are in. Allow yourself to shift one click along the dimension of ambiance. Note this movement into a new space—a macrodimensional shift—then make your move.

NOTE: If this recipe makes no sense to you, try reading one of the classics—such as the *Tibetan Book of the Dead* or the *American Book of the Dead* (if you are American, this book has been written with your cultural background in mind). After reading one of the aforementioned books, try the recipe again. If this recipe still makes no sense, skip it until later.

NOTE: In the beginning of this recipe, reference was made to ambiance as a dimension. Actually, life is not quite that simple. Ambiance is more of a conglomeration of many dimensions all rolled into one. For the moment, and perhaps a long time to come, this is sufficient. Just breaking into one new dimension is enough for now.

Get A Question Answered

To do this recipe, you will need a question. This could be a question you are currently working with, a question that you would like to work with, or a question that has been bugging you for a while. In any case, it should be a question that is real to you and you care about finding an answer to.

In case you haven't guessed already, let's make this very clear: the kind of question being referred to here is not math word problems or geography questions.

If you are unsure about the nature of the question, you could formulate the question as if you had the opportunity to speak with a television psychic, or with a spiritual teacher whose understanding you trust.

Recipe) Before beginning game play, write down your question in a journal or some other record book. After jotting down your question, subvocalize it three times. As you play the game, look for an answer or clues to an answer to your question. After the game is finished, record a brief synopsis of whichever answers you may have found during the game. And then finally record any reformulation of your question which may have come about as a result of working with the question throughout the game.

Will To Play

Unless we've had special training (or have suffered a severe blow to the head), we approach the living of this life as if we are in a time-train running along a single track starting at birth and ending at death. In addition to the assumption that we are always moving forward in time along a single time track, we also maintain the illusion, as we move from the present into the future, new track is being laid moment by moment.

We find it perfectly reasonable to reference track behind us —the past—as if it still exists and is still very real. However, we do not give the same deference to the track before us— the future—which we are about to travel.

If we think of our future track as already laid, all manner of philosophical questions, such as free will and destiny, come clambering for our attention. But, not to worry. This recipe does not require that you adopt any particular position on those questions. Consider this recipe an evidence gathering expedition.

For the purposes of these recipes, allow yourself to consider the path from the present into the future as "track that has already been laid." So rather than creating new trails in virgin snow, we are traveling within tracks that have already been made.

Recipe 1) When making your game move, get the definite

sense that you are following along track that has already been laid—sense that your move is preordained and predetermined. The track of this move has already been laid —you are just following along the track.

This recipe will probably work best with *any game* that has physical playing pieces that move around on a game board.

Recipe 2) When making your game move—following through the tracks already laid—follow along *and* contribute at the same time.

If you are a little fuzzy on the notion of *contribute,* don't worry—most folks are. Imagine you are helping several friends carry a large couch. You happen to be at the tail end of the couch. Since you can't even see where you are going, it's not your job to lead the way. Your job is to carry your portion of the weight and follow along where the couch goes.

Or, imagine that you are one of several people helping to push a stalled car. Someone else is driving the car. You and the gang are in the back, each contributing as much push as you are able. The car is so heavy that no one of you could push the car without the others. In fact, there are so many pushing the car, that you can't see the direct affect of your pushing. If you back off and don't push as hard, the car continues to move. If you double your pushing effort, the car doesn't move any faster. But, you know that if everyone pushing the car stopped contributing their portion of the push, that the car would stop.

Doorways

It is not unusual to walk from room to room using doorways as portals between the adjoining rooms. Once you accept the notion of rooms, the concept of doorways between rooms becomes obvious. In a similar sense, once you accept the notion of spaces, the concept of doorways between spaces also becomes an obvious extension.

If you asked the question, "What is a room?" The answer might be something like: "Based on our collective experiences, I'm quite confident that you have personally experienced being in a room before." Or, perhaps the answer would be something more along the lines of: "What kind of sunny beaching moron are you? Everyone knows what a mudder fargin room is. You've been in rooms before. You're in a room right now, dummy."

If you have ever used the expression, "that was an amazing space", or understood, more or less, what another meant when he or she used the expression, then you know what a space is. If you truly don't have a clue about what a space is, you could write my publisher and ask to purchase a copy of my forthcoming book *Spaces—The Final Frontier*.

Recipe) While playing any game, consider your turn to be a doorway between spaces. Just prior to taking your turn, take a snapshot of the space you are in. Then, just after taking your turn, take a snapshot of the space you are now in.

Unless something very, very extraordinary is occurring, changes in space will not be definable by changes in furniture, walls, floors, or ceilings–at least, not in the physical sense. The differences from space to space will be perceptible through changes in other aspects of the space. Be attentive to those aspects.

As you take your turn during the game, be deliberate. Take your turn as a deliberate step between spaces.

Left Hand, Right Hand

Preparation) Place your left hand and right hand on the table in front of you.

Start moving your left hand in a pattern of your choice—open/close, up/down, wiggle this/wiggle that—you choose.

Keep this going.

Now move your right hand in another pattern—any pattern—just as long as that pattern is neither the same nor the mirror image of the left hand pattern.

If all goes well, you should now have two hands doing two different things.

With some effort, it is possible to have attention on both of these hands—either consecutively or simultaneously.

Make note of the fact that even though your left and right hands are doing apparently separate, unrelated activities, they are still connected as parts of the same body.

Recipe) While playing *any game*, hold the notion that you and another player in the game are the metaphorical equivalents of left and right hands. These left and right hands (you and the selected player) move in apparently separate and unconnected patterns. And yet, you are both parts of some larger body. As you play the game, continue to be aware of you and the others as "hands" of this larger body.

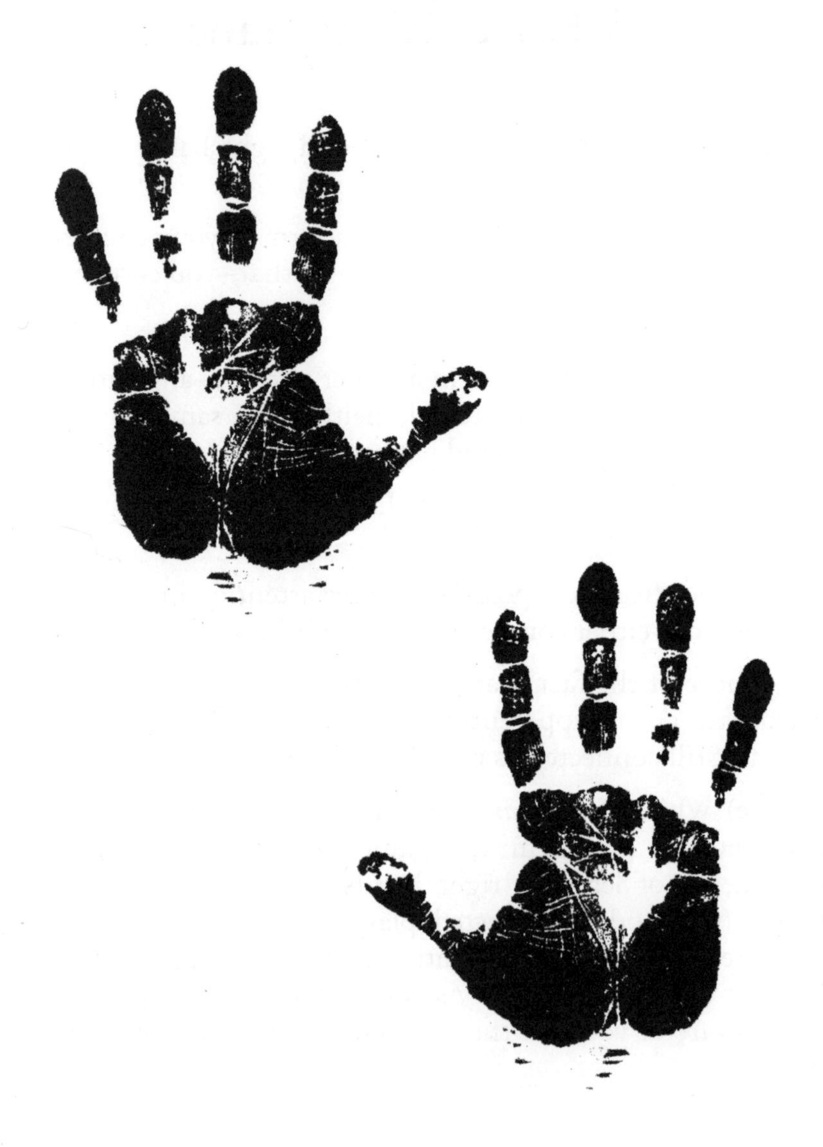

Use Alternate Hand

Sometimes a simple, almost trivial, change in activity can yield surprising shifts in perspective. This is one of those.

Recipe) While playing *any game*, use your alternate hand. If you are normally *right-handed,* play using your left hand. If you are naturally *left-handed,* play using your right hand.

This means throw dice with your other hand, move your marker with the other hand, place cards in play using your other hand.

Do everything from the opposite side. In fact, if you notice minor ticks and gestures, switch those to the opposite side as well. For example, if you have a habit of tapping your right foot, switch to tapping your left foot. If you habitually tug on your left earlobe, then tug on your right earlobe.

Sitting Like A Stone

The instructions are simple; it's just the application that's not so easy.

Recipe) During the playing of *any game*, allow your body, from the waist down, to go still. That means nothing moves, no fidgeting, no squirming, no moving of any kind. Arms, head, and upper torso move as usual. But below the waist, it is as if you were made of stone.

One might think that after making the intention to be still like a stone, it would be possible to shift one's attention to game play and simply ignore what's below the waist. Not so.

It will require constant vigilance to keep the legs *stoned*. To accomplish this effectively, you will need to split your attention, keeping a small portion of attention fixed upon your petrified legs.

If this recipe is a bit too difficult for the full course of a game, you could get an egg timer and activate the exercise during the course of one full draining of the sand. By turning the timer, you could alternate three minutes on, three minutes off.

In any case, you will eventually want to master doing this for a full hour of game play. But, don't dream this will happen the first, second, or even twentieth time you try.

You'd think with all the practice we get as couch-potatoes

that this would be a snap. Think again.

Allowing the body to veg-out requires almost zero energy. Placing the body in a condition of intentional stillness and quiet requires definite effort–effort of a type we are not used to expending.

Obviously, this recipe does not work well with games such as Twister, or Charades. Try it when playing board games or any other game played sitting around a table.

I'm A Toy

Hopefully, you have some experience with wind-up and pull-string toys. Either you've played with one as a child or you've seen one in action at the *Museum of Archaic Non-Electronic Devices.*

Recipe) Just before your turn at whatever game you are playing, wind yourself up like a toy and let it go. Instead of being a fuzzy-headed monkey banging on a tin drum, you are a toy which plays the game.

It is not necessary to mime the wind-up. Let the wind-up phase be something which you experience as part of your inner world—no need to be melodramatic about this.

Keep the Rhythm

Get yourself a metronome. This can be one of those old time wooden affairs with the brass arm that clicks back and forth, or a modern digital replacement. Given the rarity of the older wind-up wooden and brass models, I suspect most readers will opt for the modern digitals. Both will work just fine.

Recipe 1) Throughout *any game*, make your moves with rhythm—following a metronome beat. This may be throwing dice, placing chips, moving markers, shuffling, and dealing cards, or... whatever movements and gestures the game may require. Throughout the game, work to the beat.

Roll two, three, four, pick up piece, two, three, four, count your moves, tap, tap, tapitty, tap.

Recipe 2) While playing *any game*, tap a constant rhythm with your feet throughout the course of play.

Start with a simple 4/4 count, or perhaps something a bit more challenging such as an African polyrhythm or a Latin Samba.

The idea is to select a rhythm that is challenging, but within your ability—ideally, something which will not allow you to run on auto pilot.

While this foot rhythm continues, play as usual. By the way, don't be so loud as to annoy your fellow players with your incessant foot tapping.

Moment of Freedom

Apart from brief periodic moments of freedom, we spend most of our lives pushed, pulled, poked, prodded, and compelled by one impulse or another. It's like someone has clicked "GO" on a program, and then we act out the sequence of events.

If we chose to focus upon those times during which we fall forward, we could delve deep into philosophy, psychology, or any one of many other "ologies." Let's not. Instead, let's concentrate on the aforementioned "brief periodic moments of freedom"—those moments are called *Moments of Freedom*.

Moments of Freedom are brief and easy to miss, but they are also periodic. So, if you miss one, there will be another one coming around again on the guitar—just like the course of a folk song.

Recipe) When playing *any game*, wait for a moment of freedom before making your game move. This could be something such as rolling dice, in which case you'd hold the dice, and wait for a moment of freedom before rolling. Or, perhaps in a game of cards, laying down a discard from your hand, in which case, you'd hold your selected card and wait for a moment of freedom before laying it on the discard pile.

Please note: All of you wannabe perfectionists and perpetual fretters, if you demand too much certainty before rolling, you could be sitting at the table, dice in hand, until sometime next Thursday. Take your best guess. Don't overwork, fret, worry, or mangle in any of a zillion different neurotic ways this process. So what if you're wrong and you roll the dice when it really wasn't a true moment of freedom?

Be A Robot

There is something so delightfully freeing about being silly—such as when playing a game while making click-whir sounds—pretending to be a robot.

But what happens when the silly joke goes on and on and on—long after the first giggle? Or, in the case of this recipe, lasts for the full duration of a game?

If you do this recipe, you will find out from personal experience personally experienced.

Recipe 1) For the duration of *any game,* pretend to be a robot with all of the associated clicks, whirs, and jerky movements common to robots, or people pretending to be robots. (NOTE: this will have different effects when performed solo as the only participant, or as a group in which all players pretend to be robots.)

Recipe 2) While playing *any game,* in which everyone else is pretending to be a robot, you pretend to not be a robot.

Waldo

Recipe) During the course of *any game*, as you take your turn in the game, make your movements as if you are a waldo being run by someone from behind the scenes just off-camera.

A waldo is a mechanical device, such as a gripper arm, controlled by someone at a distance. When these were developed for the nuclear industry in the mid-1940s, they were named after the invention described by Robert Heinlein in his 1942 story called *Waldo*.

If the term waldo is new to you, consider the following examples:

1) A mechanical game at the arcade in which you can control the movement of a crane in the hopes of capturing a stuffed animal or other toys.

2) The mouse on your computer. By moving the mouse from side to side, you make the cursor arrow on the screen move side to side in a similar fashion. If you are using a touchpad, then movement of your finger on the touchpad is translated into movement of the mouse arrow on the screen.

3) A device used in thousands of science fiction and adventure movies to pick up and move bars of radioactive material around.

4) Devices used in deep ocean exploration submarines to pick up and collect samples.

5) The "loader" Ripley uses to fight the alien queen in Aliens II.

6) The mechanical device used by artists to trace a smaller image into a larger representation.

In these devices, movement of a control mechanism is translated into a synchronous corresponding movement of another device.

As mentioned previously, waldo comes from a 1942 science fiction story by Robert Heinlein. Here is a quote from the story *Waldo*:

"Waldo put his arms into the primary pair before him; all three pairs, including the secondary pair before the machine, came to life. Waldo flexed and extended his fingers gently; the two pairs of waldoes in the screen followed in exact, simultaneous parallelism."

If you don't know what a waldo is, find out. If you do know what a waldo is, then you are well on your way toward working with this recipe.

One thing to consider: This recipe requires a pronounced flair for the subtle.

On Stage

Perhaps you have heard about individuals and couples living in department store display windows as part of a contest, promotion, or piece of performance art. If you haven't heard of such a thing, take a moment to imagine what it would be like living in a department store window.

Recipe) As you play *any game*, get the notion that you are currently "on stage" in a macrodimensional department store window. This is a special department store with displays containing very special glass—one where the display windows are transparent to onlookers, and yet, to you appear to be solid walls.

Performance Art

White cake and yellow cake are nearly the same, except for the absence or presence of egg yolks. To some, cake is cake and there is no need to bother with both recipes. To others, the fine distinctions between different cakes is highly significant, leading to a world of gastronomic delight.

While this recipe and the recipe "On Stage" are superficially similar, they are fundamentally different. "On Stage" has been presented first, because it is best if you experiment with that recipe prior to experimenting with this recipe. It is a fruitful sequence.

After you have experimented a bit with "On Stage", then try your hand at this recipe.

Recipe) While playing *any game*, ring a bell at the beginning of your turn and then ring this same bell at the end of your turn. Use the ringing of the bell to signal the beginning of your art performance piece and the end of your art performance piece. This bell ringing formally begins and ends the art piece.

A ringer such as those used at a motel check-in counter work well for this recipe.

Wikipedia offers the following definition for "Performance Art":

"Performance art is art where the actions of an individual or a group at a particular place and in a particular time, constitute the work. It can happen anywhere, at any time, or for any length of time. Performance art can be any situation that involves four basic elements: Time, space, the performer's body, and a relationship between performer and audience. It is opposed to painting or sculpture, for example, where an object constitutes the work." (For a more complete definition consult www.wikipedia.org)

Marionette

Marionettes are fun to make and fun to use. As preparation for this recipe, it is highly recommended that you work with a marionette. Marionettes can either be purchased from a local toy store, or you could even construct one using simple instructions off the internet.

Recipe) While playing *any game*, hold the notion that your body is a marionette.

Subliminal Scenes

There are two fundamental methods for inserting subliminal messages into a movie or commercial.

In the first technique, a single suggestive frame is inserted periodically. Since the visual frames fly by at fifteen or more frames a second, a single frame is too fast to be consciously perceived, but not too fast to have a subliminal effect. Many years ago, movie theaters would slip an image of a soft drink, candy, or popcorn into a movie periodically. Hopefully, no one could detect the sneaky image, but the audience would still be influenced to buy more from the snack bar.

Another technique is to build the suggestive material into the primary content in such a fashion that it does not expose itself consciously, but it will still have a subliminal effect. An example of this technique might be a blended image of a woman's breast overlaid on a picture of an open carton of sour cream. Another example could be the almost imperceptible overlay of a woman's figure in the stream of liquor pouring into a glass. Yet, another method of fulfilling this kind of subliminal insertion is through the choice of color palette or musical background.

Recipe 1) While playing *any game*, periodically scan for subtle glitches in the stream of events which could be evidence of subliminal frames being inserted into the movie making up the game.

Recipe 2) While playing *any game*, periodically scan for subliminal messages being blended into the primary content of the movie making up the game.

In the first recipe, you will be looking for quick, almost imperceptible flashes of alternate content.

In the second recipe, you will be looking for undertones and subtle tones overshadowed by the more brash content of the game play.

Meeting of Minds

Imagine you are living in a science fiction futuristic society in which free thought is prohibited, and unapproved ideas are monitored. In such a society, it would not be possible to come right out and say something if it happened to be on the unapproved list. In such a case, you would have to find a way to communicate with others through a process of code or reading between the lines.

Or, imagine you find yourself caught in a time loop doomed to repeat the same actions over and over again and make the same conversation loop after loop after loop. Since the conversation is predetermined, and your actions are repetitions of that which transpired before, you would need to find some other means of communication if you wished to convey anything to others also caught in this same loop.

Recipe) Hold the notion that during the play of *any game,* any communication you wish to have cannot be accomplished through the standard mechanisms of speech or action. If you wish to communicate or come to a meeting of the minds with others in the space, you will need to find other means to convey your impressions other than speech or action.

This happens to be one of those recipes which can benefit from a short debriefing after the game, with others in the game, who also happen to be working with the spiritual gaming aspect of the game.

If you have chosen to work with spiritual gaming recipes in a group without letting them in on the secret, then keep the secret. Do yourself a favor and don't tell folks that you've been doing some secret exercises during a game after the fact. I've never seen this conversation go well. If you are doing spiritual gaming on the sly, keep it on the sly.

However, if you are working with a group of folks that deliberately use spiritual gaming recipes, then this is one of those recipes which will benefit from a short debriefing after the session.

By the way, did you notice the repetition of the qualifier "short" when describing this debriefing? That is not an accident. There is much to be gained by comparing notes with others. But, there is little to be gained by over-thinking, over-talking, over-philosophizing this material.

By Any Other Name

Recipe) While playing *any game,* refer to each of the other players in the game by your name.

If you are playing chess, after your turn, you might say: "Okay, Claude, your turn." (That's assuming that Claude is your name. If your name is John, then you would use John.)

Or perhaps you might be playing Monopoly and one of your opponents rolls a nine, landing on Park Place, which you happen to have a hotel on. In this case, you might say something like: "Okay, Claude fork over $1200."

If you are playing bridge, you might find yourself saying something along the lines of: "Well, Claude and Claude won that last hand, Claude was the dummy, and Claude made the mistake of leading into Claude's strong suit. Good thing Claude and Claude didn't bid a grand slam; they might have totally trounced Claude and Claude."

Since each player in the game will be referring to each other player in the game by their name, you will be getting called any one of a number of names throughout the course of the game. I suppose you'll have to pay attention in order to keep it sorted out.

Aura

In the book *Human Biological Machine as a Transformational Apparatus,* E.J. Gold describes in great detail the relationship of the machine (composed of mind, body, emotions) and the being. If you are seriously interested in the subject of spiritual development, you owe it to yourself to grab a copy of this book and read it. This book is a classic in the field of spiritual transformation. I won't do you or the book the disservice of attempting a summary of E.J.'s book. I shall just make the briefest mention of one idea related to this recipe, and leave it as homework for you (the reader) to fill in the blanks through a detailed reading of *HBM* yourself.

The point I wanted to bring into the discussion from *HBM* for this recipe is this: We each have a dual nature–having both a being and a machine. The being and the machine each have an electromagnetic field. That means that while you are sitting there playing any game, you are emanating at least two electromagnetic fields.

So how does "Aura" come into this? Well, the phenomenon commonly called an "aura" is the visual perception of the combined effects of these two electromagnetic fields.

Recipe) While playing *any game,* visualize, sense, or just be aware of the existence of the "aura" (electromagnetic fields) surrounding each player.

Plasma Ring

Note) This recipe is an extension of the recipe *Aura.* Do yourself the favor of working on that recipe before moving along to this one.

A plasma is a phase of matter distinct from solids, liquids, and normal gases—typically an electrically neutral, highly ionized gas composed of ions, electrons, and neutral particles.

One could think of plasma as an electromagnetic fluid. It flows, ebbs, swirls, and behaves like any other fluid. Granted, this is not the place for an exact physics dissertation on plasma fluids; this rough description should get you going in the right direction.

Each player's electromagnetic field will extend somewhere between a few feet up to ten feet. This means that when sitting around a table playing a game, our electromagnetic fields are interpenetrating. This touching of auras is not from physical contact of flesh to flesh—but rather from the direct interaction of the fields surrounding each of us.

Recipe 1) While playing *any game,* divide your attention and place a small portion of your attention on the plasma ring created by the overlapping auras of players sitting around the table.

When the auras of the players combine into a plasma ring, we have the possibility of energy flow around the circle. This may be clockwise, counterclockwise, alternating, pulsating, wiggly, squiggly, or whatever. For the moment, it is enough to entertain the prospect of an energy flow.

Recipe 2) While playing *any game,* be aware of the plasma ring formed by the combined fields of the players present, *and* be aware of any possible energy flow within this ring.

Super Glue

Recipe) While playing *any game,* make-believe that your left hand is glued to the table. If you happen to be a natural lefty, then make-believe your right hand is glued to the table.

In case you missed the part about "make-believe," let's review: *Make-believe* your hand is glued to the table—as in, pretend, as in, don't use real glue.

Giants

When reading *Jack and the Bean Stalk,* we tend to think of ourselves as being on the same scale as Jack. What if it is we who are the giants?

Recipe) While playing *any game*, form and hold the notion that you and your fellow game players are giants.

Last Move

As a kid, I used to love Jujube candies at the movie theater. I think there was a state law that they could only be sold at movie theaters. At least, that is the only place I recall having eaten them. Jujubes were a little like a cross between road tar and gum drops. With my allowance, I had just enough for the price of the movie and one box of candy. Thus, it was with some sense of disappointment when I finished the last of the candy. However, given the tar-like nature of Jujubes, it was not uncommon for one to be stuck to the end of the candy box hidden away. Finding such a candy stuck to the bottom of the box was always a delight. It meant one more chewy morsel.

Thing is, this final chewy bit was sweeter and more flavorful than any of the other candies in the box. Eating that last candy knowing that it was the last candy, helped me to bring more of my attention and presence into the event.

Recipe 1) Make each move as if it were your last–not the last move of the game, your last move period.

On an ocean cruise, it was not unheard of for passengers to be assigned seating in the dining room. This may have been of some benefit in the advent of an emergency, or it may have been an accidental tradition carried forward from cruise to cruise with no one understanding who started it and why it was considered a good idea in the first place. Point is, once upon a time, it was not uncommon for passengers to take meals with the same table of fellows throughout a voyage.

Imagine what it may have been like having dinner with your table of fellow passengers on that final evening before the ship reached port. Everyone at the table would know this to be the last night. After tonight they would not be seeing each other again. Before you start to well up in imaginary tears for your imaginary comrades, keep in mind that social conventions pretty much prohibit maudlin displays of melodrama on occasions such as this. Get a grip man, you've only known the other passengers for a few weeks. Tearful goodbyes really aren't demanded or called for.

Recipe 2) Play *any game,* holding the notion that this game may well be the last occasion you will spend time gaming with this group of friends.

This is not a recipe for playacting. Nor is it a recipe for exercising maudlin displays of soap opera sentimentalism.

Just play the game as if you have just found another game stuck to the bottom of the candy box called spiritual gaming with your friends.

Friendly Strangers

Friendly is good. Friendly—as in showing kindly interest and goodwill. And, friendly—as in not hostile. Kindly interest, goodwill, and not hostile—all of these things are good.

So what about the second part of this recipe, stranger?

Consider these three definitions of stranger: a) one who is from a foreign land, b) one in the house as a guest, visitor, or intruder c) a person or thing that is unknown or with whom one is unacquainted.

Stranger is neither good nor bad. Stranger is a statement of condition—neither threatening nor helpful. It is only the uncertainty about friendly and non-friendly that make an encounter with a stranger unnerving.

Often, when we somehow determine that an individual is not a threat, when we somehow calculate them to be friendly, we remove that person from the list marked stranger.

This is unfortunate. Just because someone has demonstrated themselves to be friendly, does not mean they are not from a foreign land, not a guest, not a visitor, not a person that is unknown, and not someone whom one is unacquainted with.

Recipe 1) While playing *any game*, consider each of the players in the game to be friendly strangers. Remind yourself periodically throughout the game that they are guests and visitors into the game space with you. Remind yourself that they are, in part, unknown, and that there is still much about them with which you are currently unacquainted.

Recipe 2) While playing *any game*, consider the notion that you are also a friendly stranger. Remind yourself periodically throughout the game you are a guest and visitor into the game space. Remind yourself that you are, in part, unknown, and that there is still much about you with which you are as yet unacquainted.

On the Lookout

Imagine that you and your fellow game players have been to an evening's entertainment, during which you all volunteered to be subjects for the stage hypnotist. After the performance, of which you remember nothing, the stage magician informed you that he has given each of you a post-hypnotic suggestion. The only information he will give you about the posthypnotic suggestion is that whatever it is, it will be gone in the morning. Tomorrow morning you will awaken bright and shiny with no hint of a lingering hypnotic suggestion. However, for the duration of the evening, the various post-hypnotic suggestions will be operating.

Recipe) While playing *any game*, keep on the lookout for any hint of this post-hypnotic suggestion in yourself and your fellow players.

Post-Hypnotic Suggestion

Continuing along the lines of the recipe *On The Lookout*, what if you and your fellow game players were actually subject to a post-hypnotic suggestion for the evening?

Recipe) Prior to beginning play of *any game*, have each player take on a post-hypnotic suggestion. Each player will do this by deciding for themselves a post-hypnotic suggestion which they will have running periodically throughout the game.

As the game proceeds, each player should keep an eye out for the display of any post-hypnotic suggestions by other players.

Whenever you detect a behavior you believe to be the result of a post-hypnotic suggestion, yell out *turnip,* and declare your observation. If you are correct, the player caught will own up to it and their post-hypnotic suggestion is broken. If you are wrong, then you are wrong and everything continues as is until someone else yells out turnip.

At the end of the gaming session, each player who has not had their post-hypnotic suggestion uncovered, reveals the nature of it to the gang. If the post-hypnotic suggestion was too subtle to be reasonable (such as "You will breath"), then everyone will give them the raspberries for messing it up.

Tea Party

Recipe) While playing *any game*, set a timer to go off at odd intervals anywhere from three to five minutes. When the timer goes off, each player gets up and moves one chair to the left.

The name of this game and the basic rules come from the Tea Party scene in *Alice In Wonderland.*

In the Tea Party scene, the Mad Hatter and other characters would leap to their feet, and run to another place setting at the table at odd intervals throughout the meal. At least that is how it happens in the animated version.

This recipe is courtesy of *Annex Games.*

Copy & Paste

Recipe 1) While playing *any game,* watch yourself. You will be looking for a behavior sequence five to ten seconds long which you will copy and paste throughout the game. When you detect a sequence of yours you'd like to use, highlight the behavior and copy it into your internal clipboard. Then, throughout the remainder of the game, paste that clip periodically into your behavior.

Recipe 2) While playing *any game,* watch your fellow players. You will be looking for a behavior sequence five to ten seconds long which you will copy and paste throughout the rest of the game. When you detect a sequence in another player which you'd like to use, highlight the behavior and copy it into your internal clipboard. Then, throughout the remainder of the game, paste that clip periodically into your behavior.

Be Here New

Here's another science fiction plot for you. Consider the possibility that your whole life has already been laid out from start to finish. The time line of your activity has been completely blueprinted and totally predetermined. The only exception to this are occasional time slots marked simply as "new."

It is only during those undefined periods called "new" that details are left unspecified. Hence, this is the one place that you can expand your life and live it in new and undetermined ways.

Recipe) While playing *any game*, consider the above science fiction as true and hold the notion that this game, and the time spent playing it, happens to be one of those "new" occasions. Play the game as if one of the few parts of your life left undetermined is this evening's gaming session.

The rest of your life may be robotic and carved in stone by fate, but these minutes are yours to invent as you go.

Counting Primes

Recipe) While playing *any game*, count the prime numbers up from 1 through 23, then back down to 1, then up to 23, then down to 1, then up to 23, then down to 1.... you get the idea.

Do this subvocally. There is no need to bother the rest of the players with a display of your counting prowess.

In case you're not familiar with prime numbers, here is a list of primes from 1 to 23.

1, 2, 3, 5, 7, 11, 13, 17, 19, 23

"*An integer greater than one is* ***prime*** *if its only positive divisors are itself and 1* (otherwise it's **composite**)". For example: 15 is composite because it has the two prime divisors 3 and 5.

Tap, Tap, Tap

[NOTE: This recipe has little to do with Edgar Allen Poe's *The Raven*. But, you may want to catch the movie by the same name, starring Vincent Price and Peter Lorre]

Recipe) While playing *any game*, persist in tapping the fingers on your alternate hand. Thus, if you are right-handed, you would tap using the left hand–and visa versa.

The suggested tapping is as follows:

1) Bring thumb and index finger together.

2) Bring thumb and middle finger together.

3) Bring thumb and ring finger together.

4) Bring thumb and pinkie finger together.

5) Bring thumb and ring finger together.

6) Bring thumb and middle finger together

7) Bring thumb and index finger together.

8) Bring thumb and middle finger together.

9) Bring thumb and ring finger together.

10) Bring thumb and pinkie finger together.

11) Bring thumb and ring finger together.

12) Bring thumb and middle finger together

13) Bring thumb and index finger together.

14) Bring thumb and middle finger together.

15) Bring thumb and ring finger together.

16) Bring thumb and pinkie finger together.

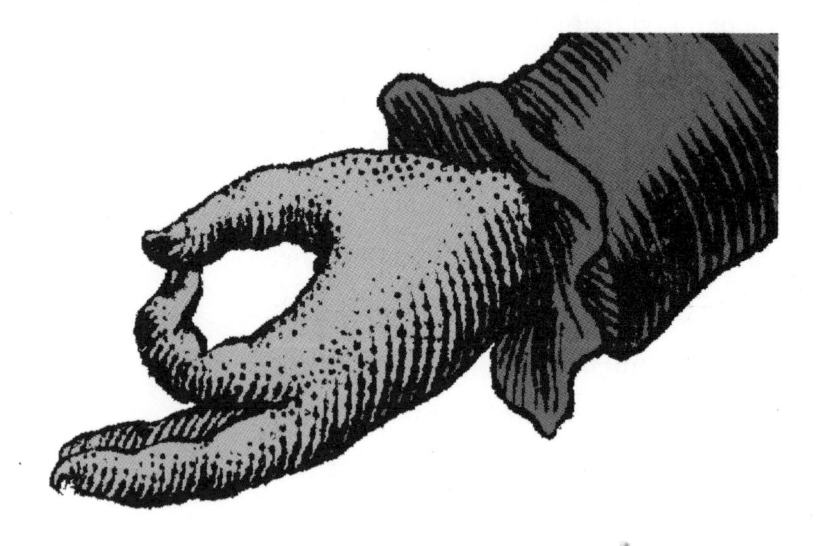

Continue the above pattern ad infinitum—or until the game is over.

When you lose your place, or simply forget to tap your fingers, don't fret, just restart.

Clown Face

This recipe requires a little preparation. Not to worry, it is well worth it.

You will need red clown noses and make-up for all players in the game.

Recipe) Play *any game* wearing full clown face make-up. Play the game as usual. The only difference being, each player is made up in clown face.

Contrary to first assumptions, this recipe is best applied to serious gaming. In fact, a major bridge or chess tournament would be ideal.

If there is an audience in attendance, they should also be in clown face.

Molasses Atmosphere

Day in, day out, we are swimming in an ocean of air. Because the air in this ocean is relatively thin, we don't notice. The air moves out of the way of our arms and legs so rapidly that we don't notice any drag or resistance from the air itself.

If we tried running in water, we would see and feel the resistance of the liquid around our legs and arms.

Imagine if we tried moving through an ocean of molasses. That is exactly what this recipe presents.

Recipe) While playing any game, move through the atmosphere as if you are living in an ocean of molasses.

Watching a group of players using this recipe while gaming is not unlike viewing Tai Chi Backgammon.

Cloning Around

Recipe 1) While playing *any game*, hold the notion that all of the other players are your clones. Yes, it is true that each of the players looks different. This is a result of the full-body masks being worn by your clones to avoid detection by the anti-clone police.

Cloning is most definitely a crime. Hence, clones take the precaution of wearing body masks to avoid arrest.

While you and your clones play the game, it might be fun to make note of the superficial characteristics you each have adopted as part of your disguise. And it may be interesting to note those behaviors which have not been masked.

Recipe 2) While playing *any game*, hold the notion that you and all of the other players in the game are clones. You are not necessarily sure which of you is the original. All you know for sure is that you are not the original. In fact, the original may not even be in the game.

When a clone is created, it begins life with a full set of memories, behaviors, and habits passed on from the original organism. Following this original moment of investment with life, a clone may develop behaviors and habits not part of the original donor host.

Recipe 3) While playing *any game*, try to uncover what about you has been with you as far back as you can remember. Which part of your behavior, attitude, habits, way of being has been there since the very beginning.

If you notice something which is of relatively recent origin, then most likely it is not part of the deeper you.

The next recipe is similar to this one presented, using a different back story.

Reincarnation Of You

Recipe) While playing *any game*, try to uncover those aspects about yourself that may be a reflection from a previous lifetime.

Negative Space

Negative space is a concept borrowed from art.

Consider a painting or photograph of a vase sitting on a table. The negative space in this image would be everything other than the vase and the table. If you are looking at an image of a house and tree, the negative space would be the visual area in between the house and the tree.

Recipe) While playing *any game*, place the focus of your attention on the negative space.

Take Your Turn

Playing a game is filled with opportunities to "take your turn." Most standard games will give you this opportunity once each round.

What if taking your turn was a post–a kind of job that we shared?

In the military, soldiers on maneuvers will take turns doing guard duty.

A large family may take turns doing the dishes.

If Atlas could find anyone else able and willing to share the load of holding the world, I'm sure he'd be more than willing to take turns.

Doctors in many hospitals take turns being on call to handle emergencies.

Policemen in television shows will take turns keeping watch on a stakeout.

Volunteers with a suicide prevention hotline will take turns manning the phone lines.

Fishermen on a boat may take turns at the helm so that others may fish.

Priests in a church will take turns hearing confession.

Firemen in a station will take turns doing the cooking.

Park rangers in a fire-lookout-station will take turns watching for smoke during fire season.

There are many jobs which require constant vigilance. Some of these jobs are so demanding that it is impossible for one individual to do it all. The job must be shared by a group of people willing to take turns.

Recipe) While playing *any game*, take turns "taking your turn."

Reactions

This recipe is courtesy of *Annex Games.*

Recipe) Draw a card from the Reactions card pile. Let all the players—other than yourself—see the card. This card will contain the reaction which players are to have to your turn. That means that during and after your turn, your fellow players will react with whatever is indicated by the card.

I've included below a short list of reactions for use in this recipe. For a larger list of reactions, consult the game *Reactions* by *Annex Games.* It comes with a very full list of possible reactions. Or, you could add reactions of your own invention.

Write these reactions on paper. If you use card stock, you should be able to shuffle and draw random reactions during the game.

Possible reactions:

Amusement

Anger

Annoyance

Appreciation

Awe

Boredom

Cool

Delight

Despair

Disappointment

Disgust

Embarrassment

Fear

Glee

Gratitude

Grief

Jealousy

Respect

Shame

Shock

Surprise

Terror

Wonder

Worry

Gratitude

Recipe 1) When playing *any game*, each time your turn comes around, be grateful that you get a turn.

Gratitude is a powerful tool. Vast possibilities open before us through the simple use of gratitude. All too often we fall into the trap of believing that we should only have gratitude when there is something we should be thankful for.

There is no reason to require that we be grateful only when we personally have something to be thankful for. That is a narrow use of gratitude, which will only serve to limit your possibilities.

Recipe 2) When playing *any game*, each time the player to your right makes a move, have gratitude that they made the move they made.

Recipe 3) When playing *any game*, each time your turn comes around, take a moment to manifest an inner prayer of thanks that you live in a time, a place, a situation which affords you the opportunity to play a game.

Some of us happen to have the extreme good fortune to be moderately free from the overwhelming demands of just scraping a living together. We also happen to live at a time in history which is marginally tolerant of alternative spiritual ideas. And, in addition to all of this, we happen to live in a time when the technology of communication is such that we can access this type of information without the grinding necessity of traveling half way around the world. We can access sophisticated spiritual teaching right in our own home. We are fortunate indeed.

Recipe 4) When playing *any game*, periodically take an inner moment to be grateful that you have the extreme good fortune to be able to pursue spiritual gaming.

Powwow

In old cowboy movies, when it came time to have peace talks there would be a Powwow. The archetypical element found in each Powwow was the passing of the peace pipe. The peace pipe was a very long stemmed pipe passed from person to person in a solemn and ceremonial fashion.

I have no idea what a real Powwow is, was, or could be, since my only source of data is old cowboy movies. Fortunately, with the advent of the internet, one can do a google search on "powwow ceremony" and find well-documented descriptions of this rich cultural event by those who know.

For the purposes of this recipe, the snapshot image of folks sitting around a circle passing the peace pipe is sufficient.

Recipe) While playing *any game*, hold the view that the passing of turns from player to player is imbued with the same ceremonial significance as would be the passing of a peace pipe.

Don't Touch Anything

Recipe) While playing *any game*, don't touch anything other than the equipment required to play the game. When you are not using the required equipment to make your game moves, you can rest your hands in your lap.

Feet On the Floor

Recipe) While playing *any game*, sit with both of your feet planted firmly on the floor. Sit flat-footed and do not cross your legs.

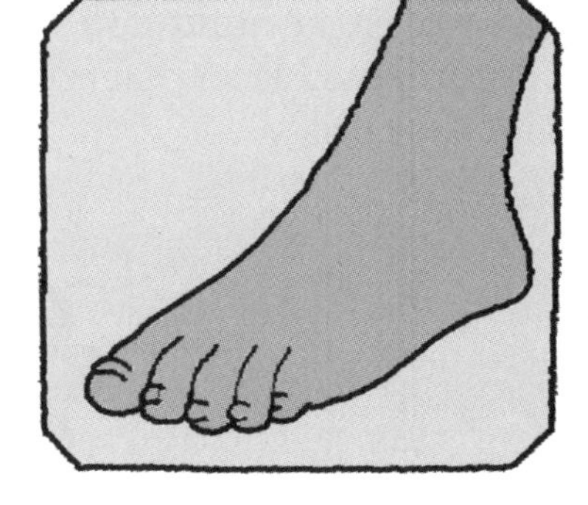

As you do this, you may notice sensations of energy flow in your feet and legs.

If any of these sensations occur, just take note. Don't worry about what should be happening. Trust me, there is no model behavior to mimic.

Just notice what's happening. Fret not about how, where, or why it should be. After doing this recipe a thousand times, you can start to ask yourself that type of question. Until then, just notice what is happening. It is worth pointing out that after doing this recipe a thousand times, you will have enough experience personally experienced to answer these questions yourself.

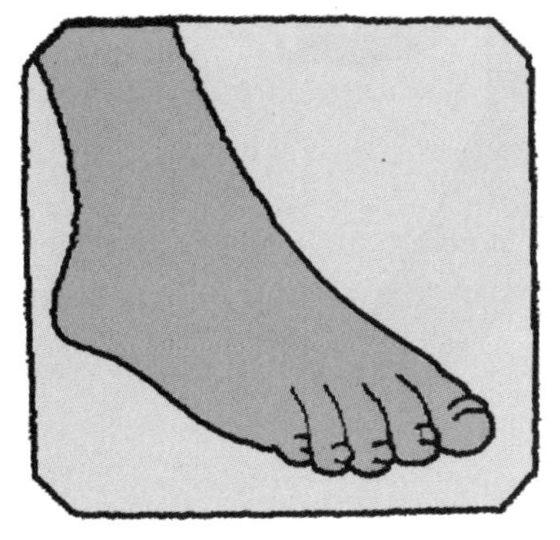

So often, if we are able to restrain our impulsive need

for instant answers, we stumble across what we are looking for around the next corner.

Don't lose a golden opportunity by feeding yourself, or allowing another to feed you, answers to your questions before you have let each question properly age. Many questions are like fine wine, they get better with age. This is not a scavenger hunt; don't feel you need to collect results as fast as possible so that you can get back to the house and claim your prize.

Peek-A-Boo

The game of peek-a-boo can be observed being played in many different cultures around the world, and if we could get into a way-back machine, we could probably see it being played from prehistory, through antiquity, into the present.

It is a simple game. One player (usually the adult, but not always) will hide from view of the other player. Then the player that is *gone* will suddenly reappear saying peek-a-boo. The second player will typically squeal with glee at this point.

Recipe) While playing *any game*, periodically throughout the game, make contact with another player and internally say peek-a-boo.

This recipe calls for a certain degree of subtlety. This is not the place for high melodrama. Just make contact, repeat internally peek-a-boo, and that's that.

This is so simple, an infant can get it. The only difference is, you are not speaking peek-a-boo aloud. You are doing it subvocally, without even your lips moving.

Sit in a Box

This recipe is wonderfully, totally beyond the fringe, delightfully stupid.

Recipe 1) While playing *any game*, each participant sits in his or her own cardboard box.

Recipe 2) If you can find a box sufficiently large, or a group sufficiently small, have everyone sit in the same box while playing *any game*.

A refrigerator box or freezer box are good candidates for this recipe.

Chopsticks and Socks

Recipe 1) While playing any game, use chopsticks to roll the dice and/or move your playing piece around the game board.

Card games might not be the best candidates for this recipe.

Recipe 2) While playing any game, wear socks on your hands.

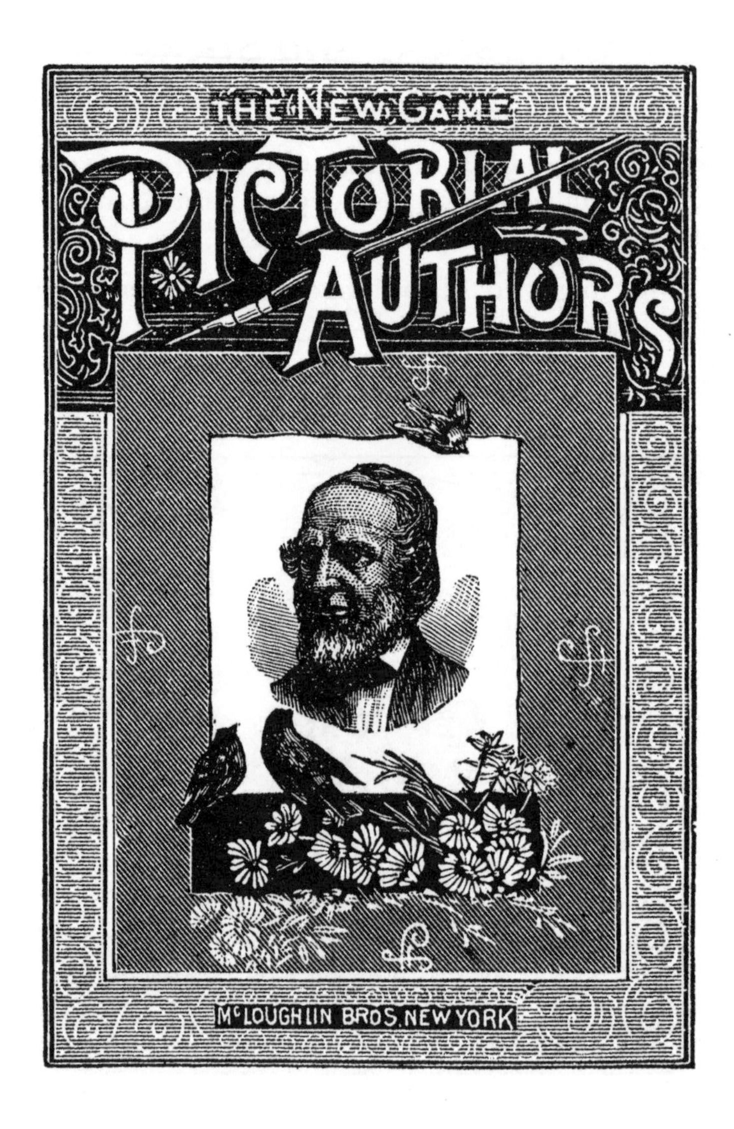
THE NEW GAME
PICTORIAL AUTHORS
M^cLOUGHLIN BROS. NEW YORK

At My Back

This recipe can be a little unsettling—but then again, spiritual adventuring, if done correctly, can be more than just a little unsettling on occasion.

Have you ever had the experience of being watched by someone from behind you? You can't see the person—they are behind you. You can't even be sure that they are still standing there—except you can feel their eyes on you from the back. This can create a strange sense of emptiness—like a voidness at your back.

Recipe) While playing *any game*, get the feeling that someone or ones are behind you watching—not watching in a bad way, just watching. Get the palpable sensation of their attention upon you from behind. Try to get a sense of this.

Some folks have reported that this recipe will give them a feeling as if there is a void at their back. You may or may not have this sensation. And any particular sensations you do have may be transient and mutate with the evolution of the recipe. Not to worry.

You may have noticed that within this book, I am very careful to not feed you any prescription of what to expect as a correct result from these recipes. There may be hints and clues about how to get on with the recipe. But when it comes to which results to expect, and which results are correct, I am as careful as possible to avoid supplying you with mine.

For you see, my results are my results. Your results will be your results. These results may or may not be the same. Right and wrong have nothing to do with it.

If two individuals were describing their experience of eating a peach—right versus wrong does not enter into it—terse versus verbose, lucid versus vague, avoidance versus engaged, attentive versus distracted, these and other measures may come into it. However, none of this should lead us to be dismissive of anyone's results.

Don't let considerations of right and wrong seduce you into dismissing a view that may open your perspective into new vistas.

This is a process and there are no brownie points given for *getting the right answer*.

Look and Listen

As any good ventriloquist will tell you, if he or she were so inclined as to give away trade secrets, the key to an effective performance is for the ventriloquist to look at the vent doll when it is talking and for the ventriloquist to listen—actually listen and pay attention—when it is talking. The more attention the ventriloquist is able to pay, the more the audience will buy the premise that the vent doll is the one doing the talking.

Some folks think the key to a good performance is for the ventriloquist to never, ever, ever move his or her lips when the doll is "talking." Posh and puff. The ability to not move one's lips is a secondary consideration. It helps, but is not the primary element to a good performance. If the ventriloquist wants us to believe the vent doll is alive, sentient, talking, and possessing of being, then the ventriloquist must believe the vent doll is alive, sentient, talking, and possessing of being.

If the ventriloquist's only thought on the subject is that he or she is merely playing a trick upon the audience, then the audience will see behind the illusion to a grown adult sitting on stage with a lump of wood sitting on his or her lap.

However, if the ventriloquist is able to suspend his or her own disbelief and open the door to amazement and wonder, then the audience may follow right along.

Recipe) While playing *any game*, look at whoever is talking—really look—and listen to whoever is talking—really listen. It's that simple.

Bring as much belief as you can to the notion that whoever is talking, is really there—really alive, sentient, talking, and possessing of being.

Talk To The Hand

If you are like most everyone I know, at some time or other you have painted lips and eyes on your hand so that you could turn it into a talking friend. Yes, I do have a rather interesting collection of friends.

Recipe) While playing *any game*, have one hand kibitz with the other before making a move. Let this hand, as a puppet, give advice to the other before each move. Let your hands have a conference at the beginning of your turn.

Be sure to speak aloud on behalf of your adviser hand. And, be sure to look and listen. Just because you have the habit of thinking of body parts as yours, does not mean they don't have something new and creative to add to the conversation.

While this may seem like a rather strange idea, you should reserve judgment. Who knows, it may turn out that your hand gives excellent advice.

Play In The Bathtub

Recipe) Play *any game*, sitting in an empty bathtub. This recipe requires that the bathtub not have any water in it. And, this recipe requires that you and your opponent be fully clothed.

These explorations into spiritual gaming are subtle and delicate. It is important that you not confuse yourself by mixing things up. To this end, it is important that you don't let this recipe devolve into a quickie in the tub.

This recipe would probably be best applied to two-person games such as Chess, Checkers, Backgammon. It's difficult to get a Bridge foursome into a single bathtub.

Playing Elsewhere

Recipe) Play *any game* anywhere other than where you would normally play.

It is hoped that you will have some common sense and avoid playing in traffic or other equally dangerous locations.

Here's a short list of possibilities:

Garage

Kitchen floor

Hallway

Backyard

On the roof

In the attic

Library

Theater lobby

Basement

Hockey field

Merry-go-round

Patio

Garden

Barn

Hay stack

Large closet

Animal cage

Sauna or Steam room

Walk-in refrigerator

Baseball park

Mausoleum

Back of pickup truck

Restaurant

Under the dining room table

Tennis court

Elevator (hopefully not one in heavy use)

This list should give you some idea of places to play other than your standard game playing locations.

Backwards

In almost any game, players take turns in a clockwise direction. The person to your right takes a turn before you, then you take your turn, then the person to your left takes a turn. All of this in a clockwise direction.

Recipe 1) While playing *any game*, take turns in a counter-clockwise direction.

Many games, such as Monopoly and Sorry, involve movement around a playing board. This movement is almost always in a clockwise direction.

Recipe 2) When playing *any game*, move your pieces in the reverse direction of normal travel around the board.

Some games use dice to determine a number; some games use a spinner. With these games, there is no rule about which direction one must spin the spinner. However, people tend to spin the spinner in the same direction each time they take a turn. This direction may be clockwise, or this direction may be counterclockwise. Whichever it is, in all likelihood, it is the same, turn after turn.

Recipe 3) Determine your normal spin direction by observing what you typically do, then reverse this direction for the duration of the game. If you would normally make the spinner twirl in a counterclockwise direction, then make the spinner twirl in a clockwise direction.

Relax Facial Mask

Recipe) While playing *any game*, let the muscles in your face relax, allowing the smile, grimace, frown, smirk, or whatever expression you would normally hold, melt from your face. Just relax the face.

When relaxing your facial mask, there is no need to be slack-jawed or weird. Simply allow the unnecessary tensions of the face to melt away.

This recipe is asking that, for the duration of one game, you allow your facial mask to fall away.

Periodically, scan your face for tension. If you find tensions, let them drop away. Keep doing this throughout the game.

You may find it helpful to relax your feet and hands. Relaxing your feet and hands has a dramatic effect on relaxing the facial mask.

Deaf, Dumb, or Blind

Recipe 1) While playing *any game*, do not speak.

Obviously this recipe will present major problems for some games. When it comes to matching a recipe with a game, it pays to be a little thoughtful. For example, Charades may appear to be an excellent game for this recipe. And, it would be ideally suited for the parts where one is miming clues. However, not speaking becomes quite a hindrance when guessing. Don't set yourself up to fail–make the effort to pair a recipe with a compatible game.

Recipe 2) While playing *any game*, wear a blind fold over the eyes.

> *Version 2a*) Have everyone in the game wear a blindfold.
>
> *Version 2b*) Pair up so that each player has a partner playing the role of guide dog or helper monkey.
>
> *Version 2c*) Have only one person in the game wear a blindfold. Take turns being the one who is wearing the blindfold.

Recipe 3) While playing *any game*, wear ear plugs.

The ear plugs will not prevent you from hearing completely. However, they will create a very definite change in the aural atmosphere.

Snap Shots

A photographer friend of mine tells a story about the late great landscape photographer–Ansel Adams. Adams focused on what he termed the spiritual-emotional aspects of parks and the wilderness. Adams was not a fan of the *resortism* attitude of the Park Service. Unfortunately, money and stupidity have won out in the long run and now we have national parks dominated by private carnivalesque concessionaires. Lament aside, the original point was that Ansel Adams was a genius at capturing the spiritual-emotional aspects of the wilderness in his photography.

According to my photographer friend, this ability was fueled by the difficulty and expense of taking a photograph. Adams did not click off a few hundred photographs, then cull though the lot looking for something decent.

When it came to taking a photograph, Adams might stakeout a potential spot for a day or two, then setup his camera equipment long before dawn so that he could wait for just the right lighting before snapping the camera shot.

Ansel Adams was like a sniper waiting in stillness and silence for just the right moment to capture a photograph.

Recipe) While playing any game, setup your inner equipment and wait for just the right moment. Then, take a snapshot.

This snapshot can be a landscape of the room. It can be a portrait of fellow players. Or, it can be a study of your inner space. Whatever the snapshot you choose to take, scout it out, lie in wait, bide your time. Then, when it comes time to grab the snapshot, do it with deliberate intent.

At the end of the game, do your best to describe the snapshot to your fellow game players.

If you do the job of grabbing the snapshot well, you should be able to describe it in a wealth of detail at the end of the game.

At the Adults' Table

When I was a youngster, there were too many folks at Thanksgiving dinner for all of us to sit at one table. So, in our family, the adults would sit at one table and the kids would sit at another.

Judging by comedy sketches on Saturday Night Live and scenes from scads of movies, this kids' table/adults' table split was not unique to my family.

Recipe) While playing *any game*, get the notion that you have finally been allowed to sit at the adults' table. This is your first time playing games at the adults' table.

Afterword

Books are funny, mutable creatures—we begin them as one thing and finish them as another. This is true for readers and authors alike.

We begin a book with raw intentions based on preconceived notions. Gradually, as we become familiar with the actual content, we mutate in a reflexive response to the book as we encounter it. This is a good thing. If reading or writing a book left us unchanged, without new answers, new questions, or expansion in our understanding, and still stuck with the same old horizons—then what's the point?

Notes on Sub-Vocalization

Various recipes throughout this book request that you sub-vocalize one phrase or another.

If the idea was to just think the phrase, you would have been asked to "think the phrase." Instead, you have been asked to "sub-vocalize the phrase." So what's the difference?

When you sub-vocalize, you engage the muscles attached to the vocal cords. This will remove the sub-vocalization from the realm of mental chatter and bring it into the realm of the manifest. It is critical that the physical be involved. Mental chatter simply does not have the same power.

How loud you speak is not important. When you sub-vocalize, it is possible to speak softly so that no one other than yourself can hear or know what it is you are saying, thus assuring you of some privacy and/or discretion. In fact, it is not even necessary to pass air across the vocal cords. The activation of the muscles is sufficient.

It is realized that even though you are not being asked to say anything shameful or profane, that you may still wish to preserve some discretion. No problem. As long as the muscles of the vocal cords are engaged, it does not matter how loudly or softly you speak.

X-Factors

Transcript from an imaginary conversation:

> *Q) Is it true that one can use standard run-of-the-mill, ordinary games such as Mankala, Parcheesi, or Diablo for spiritual gaming?*
>
> *A) Yes. I've done it, seen it, and heard tale of it.*
>
> *Q) Are you saying that everyone playing those games is doing spiritual gaming?*
>
> *A) Mostly no and a little bit yes. The vast number of folks that play games just play games—nothing special about it. Fun is fun, games are games, and it's not uncommon for folks to have fun and play games. However, there are those few individuals who, either by accident or design, play games in the fashion we refer to as "spiritual gaming."*
>
> *Q) So what's the difference? Do players have to be initiated through some special ritual or teaching? Do players need to receive some kind of special shaktipat, baraka, or other spiritual grace before they can do "Spiritual Gaming?"*
>
> *A) Nope. No such requirement. It's not that easy. Nor is it that hard. As the hunter said to his blind dog chasing a wily squirrel, "You're barking up the wrong tree."*
>
> *Q) So what makes the difference?*
>
> *A) X-Factors.*

While the above "conversation" begs the actual question, it

does serve to focus and refine the question. And, as any physicist can tell you, the answer is only as good as the question. So what are these x-factors that can transform playing an otherwise normal game into spiritual gaming?

First, before we go too far, it is very important that you pay careful attention to the use of the term x-factors, not x-factor. See the difference? X-factor**s,** plural, as in more than one. There are many different x-factors. Write down the phrase "x-factors" a hundred times and underline the s if necessary. Do whatever it takes to not allow yourself to fall into the mistaken notion that there is one, and only one, x-factor. I hope this is clear.

Second, please be aware that I don't intend answering this question to your satisfaction. I have no intention of putting the question to bed. Nothing in this answer, or any answer I may give, should be allowed to settle the question—that is not the intention. Quite the contrary. If the existence of a class of something-or-others called x-factors can be demonstrated, and if it can be demonstrated that these something-or-others indeed function to catalyze otherwise ordinary gaming into spiritual gaming, then the goal of this appendix shall have been accomplished.

This is an experimental science, not theoretical.

Consider the following "table top" demonstration as a means to open up the subject of x-factors.

Here's a simple experiment that you can do.

Spend ten to fifteen minutes being with another person...

just sitting with them in the same space. Admittedly, most will have done this many, many times before. Only this time we'd like to introduce a few conditions (or factors) into the mix.

As you sit "being with another person", add in the following:

a) Place both feet on the floor.

b) Don't fidget.

c) No touching the other.

d) Relax the facial mask. Let the muscles in your face relax, allowing the smile, grimace, frown, smirk, or whatever expression you would normally hold, melt from your face—no need to be slack-jawed here. Just relax the face.

e) No talking.

f) Gaze into the eyes of the other person. Without making this into a "staring contest" simply use the eyes of the other person as the centrum of focus for your vision.

g) Allow your vision to diffuse—i.e. relax any necessity to focus on any particular detail. Allow all data within your visual field to have the same relative importance.

If you actually do this experiment, you will notice something very different. This can be stated with confidence, based on a review of expressed results from several thousand folks who have carried out this little experiment. However, since in all likelihood you are reading this prior to actually doing the experiment, nothing specific will be said about the results–wouldn't want to spoil it by enumerating any of these experiences. Suffice it to say, the results, while subtle in some cases, were palpable and definite in all cases–and, for some, life-changing. Adding the little factors mentioned above will most definitely transform this into something that cannot be confused with sitting across the breakfast table.

How could those additional "rules", or factors, cause such a difference? Not a good question. "Why is red paint red?" This is a very interesting question with application in physics, chemistry, psychology, molecular biophysics and several other academic disciplines. It is a good question when asked in those areas. But to an artist, a better question would be something such as: "What's the deal with this red and that green? Why does it go all weird when I blend them on canvas, and more importantly, how do I duplicate that effect on rice paper?" This is an example of the kind of question that working artists may have.

So, returning to our question above: "How could those additional factors cause this difference?" a better question might be: "Which of the seven factors may be relaxed or changed?"

After performing the above experiment, you will know from personal experience personally experienced exactly what the effect of using all seven factors are.

What about changing one factor at a time? What about trying five of the seven? What happens if instead of using factor f as is, we modify it such that we are sitting back to back? Or maybe leave factors a through g as they are and just change the rule about talking? Good experiments. Great idea. Try them out. Indeed, this type of experimentation will be most productive.

> *Q) Does this mean that to transmogrify any standard gaming experience into spiritual gaming, all we need do is: Place both feet on the floor, don't fidget, no touching, relax the facial mask, no talking, gaze into the eyes of the other person, allow the vision to diffuse?*
>
> *A) It's not that simple. While the above factors would make most any event very different, you might not like the difference. For example, many people consider mint jelly on lamb to be yummy. However, would you be surprised to learn that few of those people like mint jelly on caviar? It is different. But it is not yummy.*
>
> *Q) So then, these special factors that can transform an otherwise normal event into something extraordinary are not always the same?*
>
> *A) That is correct. Sometimes the appropriate factor is one thing. Sometimes the appropriate factor is something else. It is a variable. An unknown to be solved for in each specific application.*
>
> *Q) Oh. So that is why you call them X-factors.*
>
> *A) Yes, the "x" in x-factors is a deliberate allusion to*

algebraic equations. It is used to reference unknown but definite elements of a mathematical nature.

Get the idea?

Sometimes the x-factor will be an added rule or two.

Sometimes the x-factor will be a mood, posture, or even a mentation adopted by the players.

Sometimes the x-factor will be the reworking of the games' existing rules—eliminating or redefining aspects of the game.

Sometimes the x-factor is the transformation of content.

Other times the x-factor is the transformation of the context.

There are even those occasions when the x-factor is the transformation of the pretext.

And, on occasion, the x-factor is the intention of the players that the game be a spiritual game.

By the way, don't let the fact that the x-factor varies from game to game suggest that these factors are arbitrary. Quite the contrary. Often the x-factors are very specific. Many games have special x-factors which will only work on that exact game, and no other.

Homage

My scientific training is in Molecular Biophysics. Virtually everything I've learned about Biophysics has been eclipsed by the amazing advances of the past few decades, which have been eclipsed by the amazing advances of the past few years, which have been eclipsed by the amazing advances of the past few months or weeks.

The facts of a science, and even the underlying theorems are volatile—evaporating readily into yesterday's news. The part of science which is not ephemeral is the method, or approach, to science. This has stayed with me through those same decades, which wreaked so much havoc upon the details.

One thing I carry with me from my graduate school days is an appreciation for the relationship between a graduate student and his or her graduate advisor—sometimes called major professor. As a trusted advisor a major professor can be relied upon to give direction—a most valuable asset when one is first finding their way through a complex and often occult area of study. Consider, however, that the major professor is deemed the *major* professor, not the *only* professor.

Obviously, many individuals in the field contribute to the shaping of an incubating graduate student. Even so, it is not uncommon for a writer to include author credits to his or her major professor even if there may be no direct intervention. All of this in honor of the fact that almost everything which comes from a newly hatched graduate student has been influenced in whole, or in part, by the relationship enjoyed with his or her advisor.

It would be hard for me to point to anything within this book that is not here as a direct result of my relationship with E.J. Gold. While it is true that he and I share a mutual background which includes physics as well as the field of the spiritual sciences and the science of perception, I can say without reservation that anything within this book which is not a direct encapsulation of his teachings has most certainly been influenced by said teachings.

Given that circumstances have not afforded him the opportunity to edit the material contained herein, it would be unfair to attach his name to the book as author. No point saddling him with responsibility for omissions, muddled bits and pieces, or the overly creative approach to punctuation which I seem to enjoy. Whether it is true that I enjoy creative punctuation is yet to be demonstrated. I'm not arguing the existence of said odd punctuation. I'm just not certain about the level of enjoyment.

If during your work with the material in this book you chose to attribute the good bits to E.J. Gold and the muddled bits to me, you would not be far off the mark. However, you may also want to attribute the scary bits to him as well. When it comes to unveiled visions of the void, he's your man.

About the Author

Born: 9-2-51, Sacramento, CA.
Educated: A lot.
PhD.: Molecular Biophysics.

Vocations/Avocations: Artist, writer, scientist, editor, gold miner, teacher, sculptor, painter, dancer, tree planter, programmer, web developer, jeweler, screen writer, freelance press, game designer, museum curator, and....
Let it suffice to say that I came from a very creative family environment which valued the sciences and the arts -- both equally respected as natural by-products of a creative, questing mind. I seem to recall lots of skate-boarding, bike riding, wooden sticks whittled into guns, fishing, camping, toy rockets, chemistry sets, Erector sets, broken glass mosaics, poker, tunnel forts, crystal radios, dirt clod fights, Risk, toy figures, model airplanes, Stratego, reading, reading, reading, and the ever present Mad magazine. You know... the usual.

Currently my time is spent in a kaleidoscopic scurry between writing, sculpting, programming, painting, web-design, consulting, game design, jewelry, gaming, freelance press, and miscellaneous art projects.

If the past is anything to go by, which I believe it is, then my future is pretty indeterminate–at least, insofar as specifics are concerned. Most likely I will be eternally involved in one form of creative project or process after another. What the nature of that project may be, or what the specific manifestation of this creativity will be, is left to see.

If you are wondering about other publications, below you'll find a list of books in public editions (yes, this implies books in private editions not readily available).

Handbook for the Recently Deceased

"Just Because Club"

"Everything Other Than Chess"

Partial list of games:

Zenn–3d fly-through game of zen.

Alphabet–3d player point of view alphabet trainer.

Quzzles–Quizical little puzzles (Win98)

Touch a Rock–A zen romp through repetition

Pre-Cog–Esp trainer (Win98)

gMaze–Choice Point Adventures Engine and games

Apperception–Esp and Memory trainer (Win98)

ArtDom–Fun little abstract art program. (Win98)

No22–Drumming with a difference (Win98)

Monotony–Board game.

Contact Information

Dear Reader:

If you would like to contact the book's author, or publisher, please feel welcome to use the contact information below.

We will do our best to answer your questions and supply any tools and techniques we can to help you further your own development. For a current book catalog, write to Gateways at the address shown below:

Gateways Books & Tapes
P.O. Box 370-AGC
Nevada City, CA 95959-0370

Phone: (800) 869-0658
(530) 271-2239
Fax: (530) 272-0184

Website: www.gatewaysbooksandtapes.com
www.spiritualgaming.com